meet baby animals

by seymour simon

Random House/New York

meet baby animals

CONTENTS

Most of us like to look at baby animals. We like their big eyes, soft fur, and round faces.

Most mothers shown in this book feed and care for their young. Even babies that can move around right after birth must stay with their mothers to be safe.

In this book, you'll see photos of baby animals and their mothers and fathers. You'll find out where and how the animals live. You'll discover that a baby animal is more than just a cute face!

KOALA BABY

The koala is a pouched animal that lives in Australia. It lives in the treetops and eats leaves. The koala is not a bear. It just looks like one. At birth, the baby is about an inch long and as fat as one of your fingers.

Right after birth, the baby crawls to its mother's pouch. It nurses there and grows. When it is six months old, the baby has all its fur. Then it can ride on its mother's back.

The koala mother will carry her baby until it is nearly as big as she is. After four and a half years, the koala is fully grown.

KANGAROO JOEY

Kangaroos live in Australia in some of the same places as koalas. Like koalas, kangaroos carry their young in pouches. One kind of kangaroo grows to seven feet tall. There are also smaller kangaroos that are as big as rabbits.

A young kangaroo is called a joey. A joey is only as big as a bean at birth. Like a koala baby, a joey crawls to its mother's pouch.

The joey nurses and grows in the pouch for many months. When it gets older, the joey sticks out its head to watch what's happening outside. Sometimes it comes out for a few hops. Soon the joey will be grazing on plants.

KIWI CHICK

The kiwi is a small bird that lays a large egg. The kiwi weighs as much as a chicken—about four pounds. But the kiwi's egg weighs one pound.

The father kiwi sits on the egg until it hatches. The chick is born after 80 days. It is covered with straggly feathers, and will grow into an adult after three or four years.

The kiwi is one of the few birds that cannot fly. Its long bill is used to hunt for earthworms. The kiwi lives in New Zealand, not too far from Australia, the home of the kangaroo and koala.

LION CUBS

There are usually three or four lion cubs in a litter. The newborn cubs are about as big as fully grown house cats. The cubs have stripes and spots, but these will fade as the cubs grow.

A lioness nurses her cubs until they are three months old. They cannot hunt for themselves until they are a year old.

A family of lions is called a pride. Some lionesses in a pride may have their cubs at the same time. The mothers care for all the cubs together.

Lions hunt large zebra, waterbuck, and antelope. The big cats wait near water holes and creep up to a drinking animal. Then they dash out and kill it. Lions only kill to eat, and they only kill one animal at a time.

LEOPARD CUB

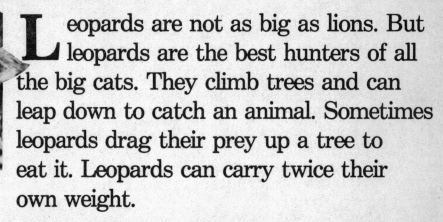

Leopards are not as big as lions. But leopards are the best hunters of all the big cats. They climb trees and can leap down to catch an animal. Sometimes leopards drag their prey up a tree to eat it. Leopards can carry twice their own weight.

This leopard cub has a silvery coat with dark spots and rings. Some leopard cubs are all black. Spotted leopard cubs and black leopard cubs may be born in the same litter.

Some people call a black leopard a panther. A leopard and a panther are just different names for the same animal. If you look at a black leopard cub in sunlight, you will see its spots.

CHEETAH CUBS

The cheetah can run faster than any land animal in the world. The mother cheetah hunts for antelope and other small animals that live on the flat plains of Africa.

Cheetah cubs are born with their eyes closed. In about a week their eyes will open. Newborn cubs have a mane of long silver hair down their backs. After two or three months, they lose the mane.

The photograph shows a mother cheetah with two cubs. They often hide in tall grass and rest. The cubs will soon learn to use their sharp teeth to kill animals for food. When the cubs grow up, they will leave their mother and live by themselves.

ELEPHANT CALF

An elephant calf is usually born at night. All the elephants in the herd trumpet and make loud noises. The loud noises may help keep away lions or tigers.

A newborn elephant calf weighs up to 200 pounds. It is covered with wool, but soon it will be nearly hairless.

The baby elephant stays with its mother for at least three years. When the calf is still small, the mother can pick up her baby with her trunk and carry it away from danger. A herd of elephants will keep a mother and her calf in the center of a circle if there is any danger.

GIRAFFE CALF

A newborn giraffe looks very wobbly. It seems to be all long legs and long neck. That's because it's five and one-half feet tall! Twenty minutes after birth, the calf starts moving around, ready for its first meal.

For its first nine months, the calf depends on its mother for food. Then the giraffe grows tall enough to feed on the leaves of trees.

Mother giraffes sometimes leave their young calves in a group. A dozen calves may be watched by two or three "baby-sitting" females. The tall giraffe adults can see a dangerous lion a long way off. The baby-sitters keep the youngsters away from danger.

MONKEY BABY

The vervet monkey swings through the trees or walks on the ground. A vervet baby holds onto its mother hanging upside down! When the monkey baby gets older, it rides on its mother's back.

A mother vervet monkey will fight to protect her young. Even if she is hurt, she will stay with her baby.

Vervet monkeys live together in groups called troops. A troop may have as many as twelve monkeys. They hunt for fruit, wild honey, insects, and birds' eggs. Sometimes they store food in their cheek pouches.

All the females in a troop may hold a new baby. But if it cries, the mother takes her baby back.

BABOON BABIES

Baboons are big African monkeys. They live on the ground. But they also climb rocky cliffs. A baboon baby must hold on just as tightly to its mother as the vervet monkey baby does. If it doesn't, it will fall off.

Baboons eat almost anything—fruits, roots, insects, and small snakes. Like vervet monkeys, baboons have cheek pouches where they can store food.

Baboons travel in troops, like vervet monkeys. But a baboon troop has hundreds of baboons! A baby baboon is safe as long as it stays with the troop. If a leopard or lion tried to hunt it, the male baboons would tear the attacker to shreds with their long teeth.

BLACK BEAR CUB

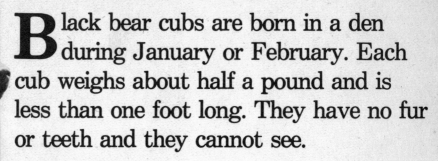

Black bear cubs are born in a den during January or February. Each cub weighs about half a pound and is less than one foot long. They have no fur or teeth and they cannot see.

The black bear cubs sleep, feed, and cuddle next to their mother for more than a month. When they each weigh four pounds, the cubs can leave the den. They are good climbers and will scurry up the nearest tree if danger threatens.

The cubs stay with their mother during their first year and part of their second.

Black bears prowl around day or night. They move through the woods looking for honey, berries, and small prey. They can swim across rivers or lakes and catch fish, too.

POLAR BEAR CUBS

Baby polar bears are born in a den dug out of snow and ice. They are born with their eyes closed and are almost hairless. They weigh about two pounds. As weeks pass, soft fur covers their bodies, and they open their eyes.

In March, sunlight shines into the den. Now the babies get their first look at the world. Their mother often carries them on her back. The cubs stay with their mother for nearly a year and slowly start hunting for themselves.

Polar bears live near the ocean. They are good swimmers and catch fish, seals, and walruses. Sometimes they eat sea plants or small land animals. Polar bears are not afraid of humans and sometimes attack them.

EMPEROR PENGUIN CHICK

The emperor penguin lays her egg on a cold Antarctic shore. Then she waddles to the sea and swims away to find food. The male penguin cradles the egg on his wide feet. His body heat keeps the egg warm.

The male walks slowly with the egg. He does not eat for months and loses a lot of weight.

The penguin chick hatches in about two months. It is covered by downy feathers that keep it warm. After the chick is born, the mother penguin returns from the sea with food. Then it is the father's turn to go back to the sea for food.

MULE DEER FAWN

The mule deer is named after another large-eared animal, the mule. A mule deer fawn has brownish-red fur covered with white spots. As it grows, the fawn loses the spots and begins to look like its mother.

A deer fawn is able to walk a few hours after birth. But it does not always follow its mother. Instead, the fawn stays in a wooded place while its mother feeds. If danger comes, the fawn stands very still. The fawn's spotted coat makes it hard for enemies to see it in the sunlight and shade of the forest floor.

MOOSE CALF

The moose is the largest of all the deer. The moose calf is not striped or spotted like other deer fawns. It is the same solid brown color as its mother.

The moose family lives in marshy places and forests. Their long legs allow them to go into deep water for food, and to reach high up in a tree to eat twigs and leaves. In summer, moose eat pond weeds and lily pads. In winter, they eat the tender tips of willows, maple trees, and other forest plants.

HORSE FOAL

The horse family includes zebras and donkeys as well as horses. Horses come in many sizes and colors. Most horses are large with long legs, long tails, and manes. Their bodies are just right for running fast. They feed on all kinds of grass and grains.

A herd of wild horses may include hundreds of animals. They usually breed every other year. The foal is born with its eyes open and can stand up soon after birth.

A male horse is called a stallion, a female horse is called a mare, and a newborn young is a foal. A colt is a young male horse, and a filly is a young female horse.

RED FOX CUB

There are four to ten cubs in a litter of red foxes. The cubs are born in an underground den. The mother nurses and cares for them while their father hunts for mice and rabbits. Red foxes also eat fruit and grass—and they may even take a fat hen from a farmyard!

A newborn fox cub has fur the color of dark chocolate, but it will grow a red coat later.

After about five weeks, the cubs come out of the den. They play together like young puppies. A fox family stays together until the young can hunt for themselves in fields and forests.

PUPPIES

Pet dogs are cousins of wild foxes and wolves. Each puppy in a litter has its own sac. The mother nibbles off the sac, and nudges the puppy close to her. The puppy can already move its head and squeak and wriggle, too!

The newborn puppy nurses right away. Then it falls asleep right where it is.

A good mother dog cares for her puppies for a few months. She licks them clean and keeps them from wandering away.

You can tell how a puppy feels by watching its tail. If the puppy wags its tail from side to side, it means the puppy is happy or playful. But if the puppy wags its tail up and down, it expects to be punished for something it did.

PORCUPINE BABY

The porcupine has few enemies. Its sharp spines, called quills, are a good protection. If a wild cat attacks, the porcupine backs up and lashes out with its tail, driving a bunch of quills into the wild cat. The quills stick in the cat's body.

The newborn porcupine is one foot long and weighs about one pound. It is larger than a black bear cub.

The porcupine baby is born with its eyes open, and it is already covered with quills. It nurses for only a few days.

Then the porcupine feeds on fruit, farm crops, and tree bark. Porcupines can walk, swim, and climb trees. But no matter how they travel, porcupines always move very slowly.

RACCOON BABIES

Baby raccoons are covered with warm fur coats. They have rings on their tails and black masks on their faces. The babies look just like their parents, except their eyes are closed.

After two months, the mother raccoon takes her young on a walk through the forest. The little raccoons follow their mother in single file.

If danger comes, the mother pushes her young up the nearest tree. Then she leads her attacker in a chase through marshes or swamps. The raccoon mother puts up a fight if she's cornered. When the danger is past, the mother returns to her babies and leads them back to the den.